A programme for Christian education in human sexuality:

Years of Innocence and Puberty

GRACEWING

Originally published in 2011
by Modotti Press, an imprint of Connor Court Publishing Pty Ltd, Australia

This edition 2011
Reprinted 2013

Gracewing
2 Southern Avenue
Leominster
Herefordshire HR6 0QF

ISBN 978 0 85244 775 8

Illustrations and design by Richard de Stoop

"To my wife, Anne, and to our children, Monica, Kathleen, Mark, Anthony and Tim, this book is dedicated - in grateful thanks for the joys of our family life."

A helpful guide
How to follow this programme

The information icon
The information icon notifies the reader of important key points that help inform and educate the parent prior to discussion with the child.

The Discussion icon
The Discussion icon notifies the reader of recommended points that help direct and engage the one-to-one discussions.
The Discussion icon always follows an information icon.

The exclamation mark
The exclamation mark highlights crucial points that ensure the parent is fully informed before engaging discussions.

Introduction: Christian Education In Human Sexuality In The Primary School

The Pontifical Council for the Family has provided guidance for parents regarding education in human sexuality through its 1995 document: The "Truth and Meaning of Human Sexuality." There are four stages of development in human sexuality described by "Truth and Meaning..." Two of them are typically found in primary school aged children – The Years of Innocence and Puberty. The educational materials and processes found in this programme are derived for this document, and attempt to assist parents in carrying out this role. A brief description and reference to the specific materials that might be used can be found on the following few pages.

The "Truth and Meaning of Human Sexuality" specifies four basic principles which should form the foundation of any programme. It is important for parents to keep them in mind. In summary, these principles are:

Principle 1

Each child is unique and should be formed individually.

◆ Each child is unique, and ought to receive individual formation, preferably from parents. It is parents who must decide (case by case) when their individual child is ready for particular information.

◆ Parents will choose the moment when they believe that their children are ready to receive instruction. This should be done in a personal dialogue: one-to one; parent to child.

◆ The person giving the instruction should, ideally, be of the same sex as the one being instructed.

Principle 2

The moral dimension should always be included in explanations.

Principle 3

Formation in chastity and timely information about sexuality must be provided in the broadest possible context of education for love. It cannot be fitted neatly into any single curriculum area.

Principle 4

Information should be provided clearly and at a time appropriate for the individual child.

◆ Parents should present information with great delicacy, but clearly and at a time they consider to be appropriate for their child's stage of development. This will vary from child to child even within the same family.

Years of Innocence

◆ Children are in the years of innocence ("latency") until the onset of puberty.

◆ This is a period of tranquillity; must never be disturbed by unnecessary information about sex. Any information should be indirect.

◆ Child is learning from adult example and family experience what it means to be a woman or a man.

◆ In a healthy family environment, children will learn that it is natural for a certain difference to exist between the usual family and domestic roles of men and women.

◆ At this stage, children cannot understand and control sexual imagery within the proper context of moral principles and cannot integrate premature sexual information with moral responsibility.

◆ "Parents should politely but firmly exclude any attempts to violate children's innocence because such attempts compromise the spiritual, moral and emotional development of growing persons who have a right to their innocence." Truth and Meaning of Human Sexuality. (Pontifical Council for the Family. 1995)

◆ A problem arises when children receive premature sex information from the media or from their peers. In this case, parents will have to give limited sexual information, usually to correct immoral and wrong information or to control obscene language.

◆ Parents must protect their children, first by teaching them a form of modesty and reserve with regard to strangers, as well as by giving suitable sexual information, but without going into details that might upset or frighten them.

 # Puberty

◆ There is a very wide variety among individual children regarding the start of puberty. Some show the first signs as early as eight years of age – others as late as fourteen years. Once the child has clearly entered puberty, it is time to begin to give more detailed explanations about human sexuality.

◆ Use your own discretion as a parent to decide on what your child is ready to handle. The Activities provided are there as a guide – not as a requirement.

◆ Formation during puberty should be considered under the following aspects:

◆ **What is the nature of a human person?**
◆ **Change & Development in the Human Body: Puberty**
◆ **Marriage & the Family, Friendship and Vocation**
◆ **The Gift of Fertility**

1. What is the nature of a human person?

This section should not be passed over. It is extremely important in setting the right context for the discussion. It also allows the parent and child to "ease into" the topic which can at first be difficult for both child and parent.

◆ "Parents should remind their sons and daughters about God's gift, received in order to cooperate with Him in bringing new life into the world." - from "Truth and Meaning of Human Sexuality".

2. Change & Development in the Human Body:

◆ "Beginning with the changes which their sons and daughters experience in their bodies, parents should give more detailed explanations about sexuality." - from "Truth and Meaning of Human Sexuality".

◆ With children individually (as needed) parents can identify the physical, social and emotional changes that are common to both sexes, and those that are specific to girls and boys, during puberty.

3. Marriage and the Family, Friendship and Vocation

◆ "Any presentation of genital aspects of sexuality should be done in the context of marriage and the family." - from "Truth and Meaning of Human Sexuality".

◆ Instruction for both girls and boys should aim at pointing out the value of motherhood and fatherhood, the reality of procreation, and the meaning of virginity.

◆ A study of the various levels of friendship allows children to reflect on the meaning and value of their own experience of relationships based on Aristotelian categories – utility friends, pleasure friends and true friends.

4. Change and Development in the Human Body: Fertility

Girls

"Parents should follow the gradual physical development of their daughters and help them to accept the development of their femininity in a bodily and spiritual sense. Normally, the cycles of fertility and their meaning should be discussed. Girls should also have some understanding of the development that is taking place in boys during puberty." - from "Truth and Meaning of Human Sexuality"

Boys

Boys must be helped to understand the stages of physical development of the genital organs. Boys should also be given some understanding of female sexual development, particularly the cycles of fertility.
- from "Truth and Meaning of Human Sexuality"

Boys & Girls

In this phase [puberty], education in human sexuality is also concerned with the genital aspects.

Faith and Ethics

Faith and Ethics Part 1: The Nature of Love

◆ Identify and give basic explanations for the sixth and ninth commandments:

6. You shall not commit adultery.

9. You shall not covet your neighbour's spouse.

◆ Explain that marriage was instituted by God. The sacrament of Marriage is exclusive and for life.

Faith and Ethics Part 2: Good Reasons For Believing As We Do

◆ In answering children's questions, parents should give good reasons for chastity and show the weakness of theories and ideas that encourage permissive behaviour.

◆ Boys and girls at puberty are particularly vulnerable to emotional influences. Through dialogue and the way they live, parents should help their children resist negative outside influences.

◆ "Parents should teach their children the value of Christian modesty, moderate dress. Parents should explain that a mature personality does not feel the need to follow every trend." - from "Truth and Meaning of Human Sexuality".

Faith and Ethics Part 3: Issues To Talk Through

◆ Even if they are socially acceptable, some habits of speech and conduct are not morally correct and represent a way of trivializing sexuality, reducing it to a consumer object.

◆ "Through an open dialogue, parents can guide their sons and daughters when they face emotional difficulties and support the value of Christian chastity." - from "Truth and Meaning of Human Sexuality".

Human Person

Human Person

Parents should remind their sons and daughters about God's gift, received in order to cooperate with Him in bringing new life into the world.

Aim: Help the child to understand God's gift to them of human life and personhood.

The Ladder of Life
◆ An explanation of the value of the human person.
◆ What makes a person – a nature that can think and choose.
◆ Why animals are not persons.

We Are Unique
◆ The human person is unique – both spiritual and material.
◆ The human person is unique – the bridge between the spiritual and material.

Love Is What God Does
◆ God is love.
◆ Jesus came in a body like ours and showed us how to show God's love using a material body.
◆ Jesus commanded us to love as he loved.

Human Persons Show Love Through Their Bodies
◆ Every act of love is God-like
◆ It is freely chosen
◆ It is a gift of yourself
◆ The corporal (bodily) works of mercy

The Human Person - A Material and Spiritual Being
◆ The human person can "know" and "love".
◆ Relationships with others is part of what it means to be human.
◆ We are created in the image of God.

Bible Study: Image of God

Points to bring out

All of these activities are intended to start and continue a conversation between parent and child. It is not necessary to complete the activity sheet if this does not suit your child – the important thing is the conversation.

Purpose: To be clear about the difference between animals, plants and humans. [Animals, plants and humans are capable of sexual reproduction. But animals and plants are not capable of true love, since they do not have the spiritual abilities of mind and will.

Therefore sexual reproduction in animals and plants has nothing to do with love. This will become clearer as we go along.]

Have the child read through the frame.

Tell the child that person is a very important concept.

A person is one who can think and choose; know and love.
To be truly happy, they need to be with others like themselves.
Because we can think, we are able to know the truth.
Because we can choose freely, we are capable of love.

Ask why rocks aren't persons.

[Answer: They cannot think or choose.]

Ask why animals aren't persons.

[Answer: Animals are not persons because they can't think in the same way that we do. They can only respond to things that they perceive through their senses. Animals don't have wills like ours – they always act by instinct. Animals cannot go against their instincts.]

Ask why humans, angels and God are persons.

(They can look at the boxes again to get some ideas!)
To be understood properly, you will need to go over this material a number of times. Opportunities for talking about this should be taken as they come up during ordinary activities and conversations. You may also like to use the cut out materials in the appendix of this book.

The child may raise questions that you can't

answer. This would be a good opportunity to bring others into the conversation – a parish priest or a knowledgeable friend.

 The Ladder of Life

What is a person? An individual with a nature that can think and choose; know and love. Persons need to give themselves to other persons to be truly happy.

God is three persons (the Holy Trinity)
Father, Son and Holy Spirit

Not Alive.	Alive.	Alive.	Alive.
	Can grow, feed, & reproduce,	Can grow, feed, & reproduce	Can grow, feed, & reproduce
		Can see, hear, smell, taste, touch.	Can see, hear, smell, taste, touch.
			Can think and choose. Is a person.

Human beings are persons. We have minds – We can think and we know that we are thinking. Our thinking leads us towards understanding why things are the way they are.

We have wills – we can choose to do what is right even when it is hard. This makes us able to love – without being forced. We are happiest when we give ourselves to others and gratefully receive what others give to us.

Animals are not persons. Animals can't think in the same way that we do. They can respond to things that they perceive through their senses . Animals don't have wills like ours – they always act by instinct.

Points to bring out

Purpose: To point out that human beings are unique.
We are persons (like angels and like God)...
.... but we are also made of matter like plants and animals.
Therefore we belong to both the spiritual and material worlds.

Look through the description of each kind of being.

Tell the child that person is a very important concept.

Human beings are unique because they belong to both the spiritual world and the material world.

Ask your child to say why human beings are like plants and animals.
[Answer: Humans are physical beings – made of matter.]

Ask your child to say why human beings are like angels and like God himself.
[Answer: Human beings are persons – able to know what is true and love what is good. They need to share their lives with other persons in order to be happy].

Point out that human beings are like a bridge between the spiritual world and the material world.

It would be useful to complete the name matching activity to reflect on the meaning of each description.

We Are Unique

Belong only to the material world.
Can be seen and touched.
Can grow, feed, reproduce.
Cannot see, taste or hear.
Are not persons.

Belong only to the spiritual world.
Have no bodies.
Cannot grow, feed, reproduce.
Do not have senses like ours.
Can know truth and love what is good.
Are persons.

Belongs to the spiritual world.
Have no bodies.
Son became a man.
Created all things, seen and unseen.
Can know truth and love what is good.
Is/ Are persons.

Belong only to the material world.
Have bodies.
Can grow, feed, reproduce.
Can see, hear, taste, touch, taste and smell.
Are not persons.

Belong to the material and the spiritual world.
Have bodies.
Can grow, feed, reproduce.
Can see, hear, taste, touch, taste and smell.
Can know truth and love what is good.
Are persons.

Human persons are the bridge between the material and spiritual worlds.

Points to bring out

Purpose: To show that human beings are meant to be like God in the way they love.
To see Jesus as the one who showed human persons what they are meant to be like.

Start by numbering each caption to match the correct picture.
Ask your child when God became a man.
[Answer: At the Annunciation, when the angel asked Mary to be the mother of God.]

Move on to the second picture.
Ask if Jesus stopped being God because he became human.
[Answer: No, at the same time, Jesus was (and still is) fully God and fully human.]

Look at the third picture.
Jesus gave to all of us a new commandment.
Ask your child what it was.
[Answer: Love one another as I have loved you.]

Look at the fourth picture.
Tell your child that we have been created in the image of God. Ask: "What is God like?"
[Answer: Jesus told us that God is love; love is what God is and does. "God is love." 1 John 4:8.]
So what are we meant to be like?
[Answer: We are meant to be like God in the way we love.]

Look at the fifth picture.
Did being human stop Jesus from loving the way God does?
[Answer: No. As a human person, Jesus showed love by what he did through his body.]

Look at the sixth picture.
Tell your child that it gives us some ways to show love using our body. Then move on to answer the questions in the box.

 # Love is what God does

Love Is What God Is... Love Is What God Does...

◯ He told us some ways of doing this.

◯ God became a man.

◯ He told us what God is like.

◯ Jesus showed us that we can love like God using our body.

◯ He came to us with a body just like ours.

◯ Jesus gave us a new commandment: "Love one another as I have loved you." John 13:34

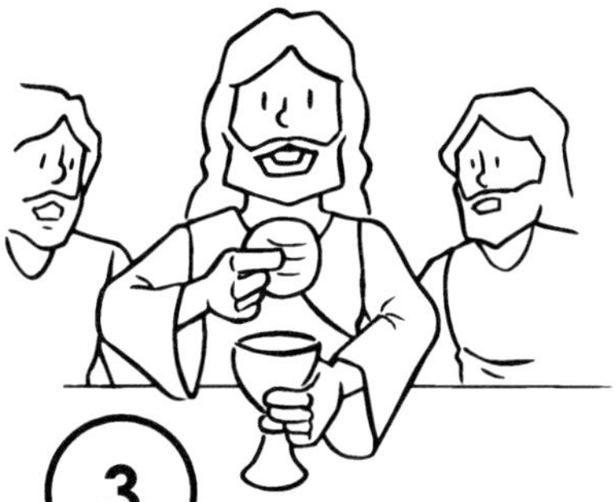

Jesus shows us that it is possible for human beings to be like God in the way they love.

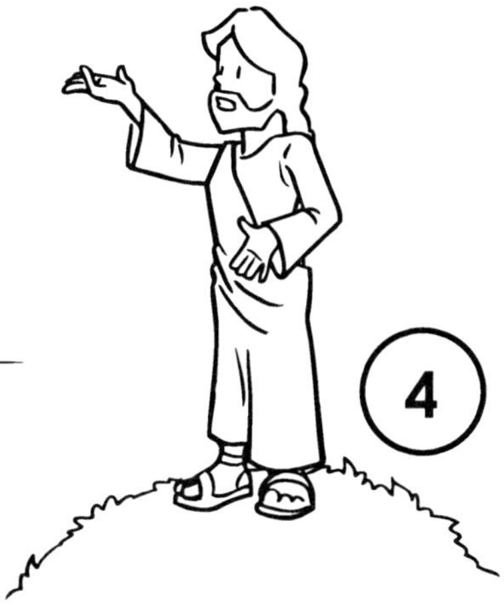

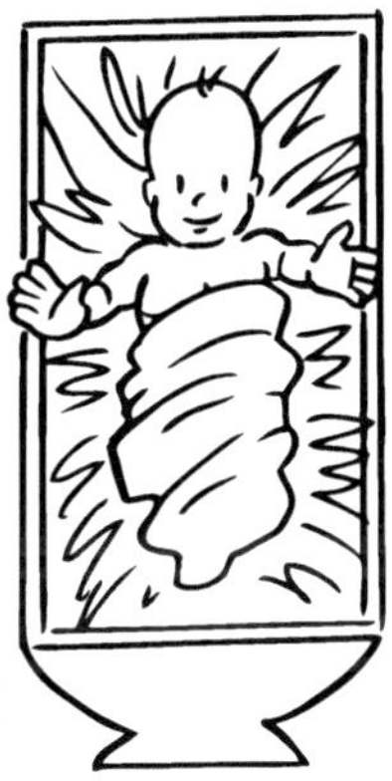

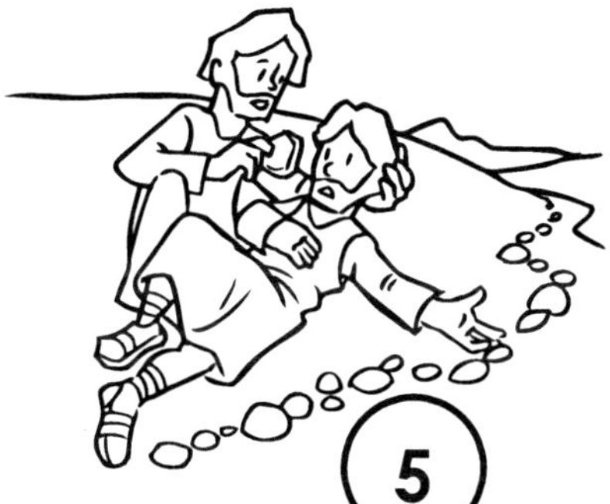

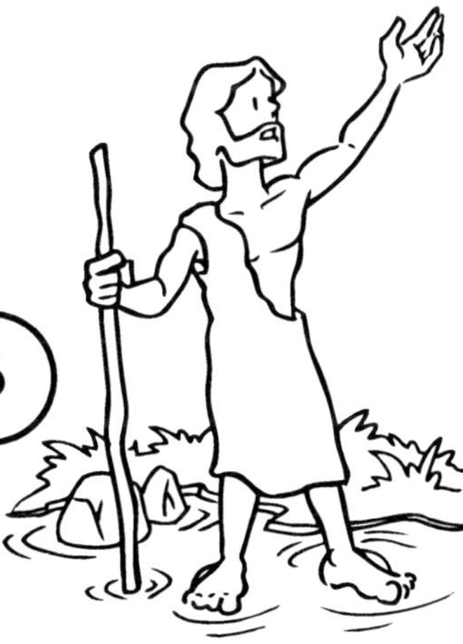

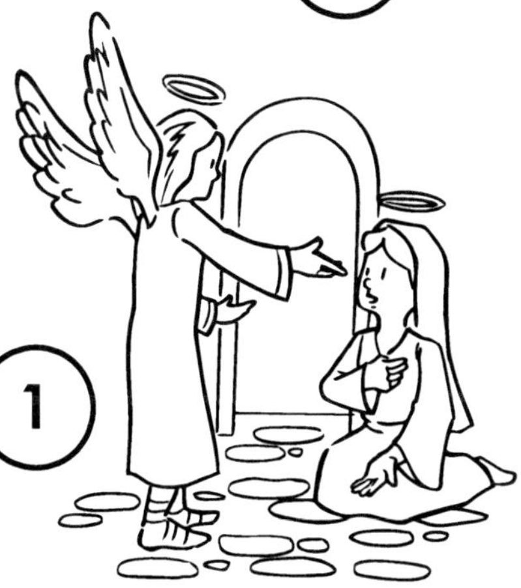

Points to bring out

Purpose: To reinforce what was learned in the previous activity
- That human persons show love through their bodies.
- To explore the meaning of true love.
To lay the foundation for teaching the meaning of our sexual powers as a way of showing love through our bodies.

Tell your child about what has already been learned in the last activity:

1. Human persons are not spirits – we are "rational animals". This means that when we show love, we use our bodies.
2. We are meant to be like God in the way that we love. Jesus has shown us how to do this.

Tell your child that every time we show love in any way, we are acting in the same way that God does.

Every act of love must be freely chosen. Every act of love is a gift of yourself. If it isn't like this, then what you are doing isn't love.

Ask your child whether animals can show true love.

[Answer: No they can't. An animal will always act according to instinct. An animal is not free to choose how it will act.]

The pictures in this activity represent the traditional corporal works of mercy described by Jesus (Matthew 25:35-37).

Tell your child that they describe some ways that we can show love using our bodies.
Have them place a tick above the ones that they have already been able to do.
(Later, it will be shown how our sexual powers are another way of showing love with our bodies.)

Work through the questions and discussion issues.

[Answers: The best gift you can give is yourself.
You can't force somebody to love you. You have to be free to be able to love.
True love can't be selfish because you have to want the good of the other person ahead of your own.]

* Corporal means "having to do with the body".
It comes from the Latin word "corpus" meaning body.

 # Human Persons Show Love Through Their Bodies

Every act of love is God-like.
It is freely chosen,
It is a gift of yourself.

CLOTHE THE NAKED

DRINK TO THE THIRSTY

BURY THE DEAD

Place a tick beside the works of love that you have been able to do.

Write one other way that you can show love

_____

FEED THE HUNGRY

VISIT THE SICK

VISIT THE PRISONER

SHELTER THE HOMELESS

Discuss: What is the best gift you can give?
Why can't you force somebody to love you?

Points to bring out

Part 1.

◆ The human person is said to be created in the Image of God – but what does this mean? The Church's understanding is that the Holy Trinity serves as the basic model for what a human being is... that is, human beings share three faculties of the Trinity:

  o Intellect: Knowing and understanding
  o Will: Choosing and loving
  o Relationship: We are more than just individuals; part of who we are is found in our relationships with others.

◆ All human beings, no matter how good or flawed in character, share in these characteristics and this is why everyone has the same human dignity.

◆ Christians try to go beyond this description and by means of the grace of God working in their lives, they try to become more like Christ - the "Likeness of God".

◆ In a human being, these three faculties are integrated with a material body. Christ is our model of what this looks like in a human person. (Our Lady and the saints show us some of the many variations that are possible.)

 # The Human Person: A material and spiritual being

**All spiritual beings
(God, Angels and Human Persons)
have three things in common.**

1. They can think, and also understand things.

They "know that they know".

The Holy Trinity is the "model" for human beings...

(Each person of the Trinity can know, and love...
and each Person of the Trinity is in relationship with others.)

This is why we can say that we are created in the "Image of God".

2. They have a will, and so they can choose to love.

They can do what is right, even when it is hard.

3. Their relationship with other persons is part of who they are individually.

This means that they can share their gifts of knowing and loving with others who appreciate it.

Jesus is God and He became man. He shows us what a human person is meant to be like.

Jesus shows us how we can best use our gifts of mind and will, as well as our bodies to become more like God.

Points to bring out

Bible Study 1: Background.

◆ In the first passage, it seems that it is the three persons of the Trinity who are working together in the act of creation ("Let us make man in our own image, after our likeness"). The movement to the singular "He created them" indicates that the three persons are acting together as one. - (See if the child can come to this understanding without help.)

◆ "Male and female He created them" indicates that the difference between the sexes is intended by God – it can be seen in all of living material creation; plants, animals and human beings are divided into two sexes.

Bible Study 2: Background.

◆ Human beings are unique because they are both spiritual and physical. A soul without a body is incomplete; this is one of the important things that the doctrine of the "resurrection of the body" teaches us:

• When Jesus rose again, His body and soul were united once more, and remain so forever.

• When Mary went to Heaven at the Assumption, it was with her body and soul.

• Human beings cannot be happy as any other form of life – they cannot become angels; this is not God's plan for them...

• Nor is it possible for any human being to be happy if they were to be changed into an animal, and nor is it possible for a man or a woman to be truly and permanently happy by pretending to live the life of the opposite sex.

• Happiness can only be found by accepting God's plan for our lives and living it out as fully as we can.

Bible Study 1

Then God said, "Let us make man in our own image;
after our likeness... So God created man in his own image,
in the image of God He created him, male and female he
created them."

Genesis 1:26-27

This passage describes the creation of human beings. Think about these things...

1. Who is "speaking" in this passage, and why do you think the passage starts using the plural (let *us*... after *our* likeness...) and then returns to the singular *(He created them.)*?

2. As well as being created in God's image, what extra characteristic do human beings have... Is this a good thing or perhaps a mistake? Why do you think so?

Bible Study 2

"Then the Lord formed man of dust from the ground,
and breathed into his nostrils the breath of life;
and man became a living being."

Genesis 2:7

The Catechism of the Catholic Church tells us that in this passage, the dust represents what is *material*, and the breath of life represents the *spiritual* aspect of human beings.

1. God created human beings to be both spiritual and physical. Do you think that God is happy with his "design" for human beings? Why?

2. Does Jesus have a body right now? Does Mary? Will I be always both spiritual and physical, even in heaven?

3. Do you think the spiritual and physical parts of human beings can be permanently separated? When will the body and soul be reunited?

4. Do you think you could be happy as an angel? Why might God have created you as a human being and not an angel?

Changing and Growing - Puberty

Changing & Growing

Some helpful hints to parents

◆ A good starting point for explanations about genital sex comes with the changes the boy or girl experiences with puberty. By answering the "Why is this happening?" questions, you have a natural lead into the things that need to be talked about.

◆ Keep in mind that you are not just giving information about biology – you are talking about what it means to be human. For that reason, you should include in your discussion the items talked about in the other sections of this booklet. Anyone can give a science lesson – it takes a loving parent to form and nurture a human being.

◆ Every child is different. The parent is in the best position to decide when to begin this instruction. Some children are now moving into puberty much earlier than was the case in previous generations.

◆ Some children want more information than others – you need to judge for yourself how far you should go at any particular time.

◆ Instruction is best handled by the parent of the same sex as the child.

◆ Look for the teachable moments – it will be easier if the child asks spontaneously; but if this doesn't happen, you may need to bring up the topic yourself.

◆ Let your children know that it is okay for them to ask you things about sex. Let them know that you would prefer for them to ask you than somebody else.

◆ The activities provided here give a basic explanation of the topic. It is good to have a access to other materials.

Changing & Growing Part 1: Puberty

◆ *In this phase, education in human sexuality is also concerned with the genital aspects.*
◆ *Beginning with the changes which their sons and daughters experience in their bodies, parents should give more detailed explanations about sexuality.*
◆ *With children individually (as needed) parents can identify the physical, social and emotional changes that are common to both sexes, and those that are specific to girls and boys, during puberty.*

Some Helpful Hints To Parents
◆ Starting points.
◆ Importance of talking about what it means to be human.
◆ Every child is different.
◆ How much information?
◆ Teachable Moments
◆ Let them know you are available
◆ Resources

Stages of Puberty (Girls)
◆ Chart of the stages of puberty in girls.

Stages of Puberty (Boys)
◆ Chart of the stages of puberty in boys.

# Points to bring out

Puberty Chart – Girls

◆ This summary table of the changes occurring in girls during puberty is taken from "Teachable Moments" by Julianne Whyte and Lisa Brick. It is It is simple, accurate, comprehensive and written in accordance with Catholic teaching.

◆ Have your child read through the chart (or read it to the child).

◆ Ask your child where he/ she thinks they fit at this time.

◆ It would be helpful to let your child keep a copy of this chart to refer back to.

Changing & Growing

Some Important Information About Puberty

Stage	Changes in Girls
Stage 1	There is no outward sign of development. Hormones start to be secreted from the brain (pituitary gland). You may feel different, perhaps a little more tired.
Stage 2	The hormones start to affect your body shape. Your breasts may start to grow, and your nipple area will enlarge. Your height and weight will increase very rapidly, and you may notice your hips look more rounded. This is because fat is being redistributed and deposited onto your hips. You will start to develop some fine pubic and underarm hair.
Stage 3	Breast development continues, and the pubic hair continues to grow. It thickens and becomes coarse and curly. Towards the end of this stage you may start to menstruate. You may become aware of some mucus discharge, or sensation of mucus at the vulva.
Stage 4	If you have not started to menstruate yet, you will be doing so by the end of this stage. Ovulation may occur in some cycles. Body hair continues to grow and thicken and hip development continues.
Stage 5	This is considered to be the last stage of puberty. You should have a fully developed reproductive system, be fertile and look like an adult female. You will have now reached your full height. You should be ovulating and menstruating regularly. This stage may not be completed until well into your 20's.

(from "Teachable Moments" by Julianne White & Lisa Brick)

Points to bring out

Puberty Chart – Boys

◆ This summary table of the changes occurring in boys during puberty is taken from "Teachable Moments" by Julianne Whyte and Lisa It is simple, accurate, comprehensive and written in accordance with Catholic teaching.

◆ Have your child read through the chart (or read it to the child).

◆ Ask your child where he/ she thinks they fit at this time.

◆ It would be helpful to let your child keep a copy of this chart to refer back to.

◆ You may like to use the materials in the appendix to reinforce the information provided.

Changing & Growing

Some Important Information About Puberty

Stage	Changes in Boys
Stage 1	There is no outward sign of development. Hormones start to be secreted from the brain (pituitary gland). You may feel different, perhaps a little more tired.
Stage 2	The hormones start to affect your body shape. The testicles, scrotum and penis continue to grow larger. The scrotum starts to develop a wrinkled appearance. You will start to develop some fine pubic and underarm hair.
Stage 3	The testicles, scrotum and penis continue to grow larger. Body hair continues to grow and becomes thicker and coarser. Shoulders start to broaden and muscular development continues. You start to grow taller and your voice deepens – this is due to a thickening of the thyroid cartilage around the voice box.
Stage 4	Your voice continues to deepen. Pubic and underarm hair continues to grow and thicken. Hair starts to grow on your face and chin.
Stage 5	This is considered to be the last stage of puberty. You should have a fully developed reproductive system, be fertile and look like an adult male. You may continue to grow in height, but many men have finished growing. **

** When a person starts or finishes puberty is entirely individual. Each person has their own biological clock that determines when these events will happen. For most people, this can take many years – until into their 20's.

(from Teachable Moments by Julianne White & Lisa Brick)

Vocation, Marriage & Family

Vocation, Marriage & Family

> ◆ *Any presentation of genital aspects of sexuality should be done in the context of marriage and the family.*
> ◆ *Instruction for both girls and boys should aim at pointing out the value of motherhood and fatherhood, the reality of procreation, and the meaning of virginity.*

The Love In Human Families Is Meant To Be Like God's Love
◆ God's love is free, permanent, unselfish, has no limits & shares his life.
◆ Human persons are called to love in the same way that God does.

Friendship
◆ The types of friendship according to Aristotle:
   Utility friends; Pleasure friends; True friends; Review.

Married Love
◆ Married couples make a free choice to love one another the way God loves.
◆ Sexual intercourse is the physical sign of an inner reality.

Loving The Way That God Does
◆ Comprehension sheet bringing together the nature of love in marriage.

Motherhood and Fatherhood
◆ The power to give new life is a great gift of God.
◆ Only human beings give new life to persons.
◆ Virginity and its meaning.

Should Everyone Be Married?
◆ We are all called to love God differently.
◆ Married people show the love of God in marriage.
◆ Priests & religious give their love directly to God.

Vocation: My Calling In Life
◆ Everyone has a call from God.
◆ How will I know my vocation?

Points to bring out

Purpose

To explain that God is a community – a "Communion of Persons" and that the love the persons of the Holy Trinity have for each other is meant to be the model for the way families live. To talk about some of the features of true love:

◆ Start by pointing out the first diagram (the three pointed arrow). Ask your child what word best describes what God is like. [Answer: Love.]

◆ Point out the picture of the crucifixion, and then go to the box on the other side of the page. Tell your child that the way Jesus acted showed us what the love of the Holy Trinity must be like.

◆ Have your children read the words in the box, and try to explain them in their own words.

Answers:
Love is given freely – it is not forced.
Love is permanent – it lasts forever.
Love is unselfish – it makes a gift of itself and does not demand anything in return.
Love has no limits – it never stops.
Love is always a gift of yourself to another.

◆ Now look at the next page. Tell your child that our human family is meant to show the same kind of love found in the Holy Trinity. The more a family shows love, the more it will be like the Holy Trinity – and the happier it will be.

◆ Ask your child the questions in the box in the bottom right hand corner.

[Answers: Yes, Jesus came to show us this kind of love.
We know that our love is true love when it is free, permanent, unselfish, unlimited and is a gift of yourself.]

God

The Love In Human Families Is Meant To Be Like God's Love

When God loves, the Persons of the Trinity live the kind of life they are meant to live

Jesus showed us what God's love is like:
Free
Permanent
Unselfish
Unlimited
Gift of Self

Human Persons

When we love, we also have the power to give life

When I love, I live the kind of love I'm meant to live

When we love truly, it will be the same kind of love that Jesus showed us:
Free
Permanent
Unselfish
Unlimited
Gift of Self

> **What do you think?**
>
> Are human persons meant to love in the same way Jesus did?
>
> How can we tell when our love is true love?

37

 # Friends

This description of the three kinds of friendship is based on the work of the ancient Greek philosopher, Aristotle.

Utility Friendships (User Friends)

◆ User friends use you for what they can get out of you.
◆ If you stop being useful, you will stop being their friend.
◆ User friends give just enough to keep the friendship going, but they are mainly interested in taking what you have to offer them.

Discuss.

What kinds of things would a utility friend be interested in you for?
When might it be okay to have utility friends?
Can you think of some examples of utility friends in movies or TV?
Can God be a utility friend? Why?

 # Pleasure Friends

◆ Pleasure friends are your friends only because they find some pleasure in being your friend.

◆ A pleasure friend might love some special quality in you: you might be good looking, funny, good at sport etc. But if that quality disappears, or if the friend stops finding it pleasurable, the friendship will cease.

◆ A pleasure friend won't let you be yourself – you have to be showing them the quality they like all the time or they won't be your friend!

◆ Most young children only have pleasure friendships. As they grow and change, so do their friendships. This is normal.

◆ Some teenagers and even some adults never grow up in the way they act towards their friends! They remain immature and self-centred.

◆ Some people who seem to have lots of friends only have pleasure friends or utility friends.

Discuss.

◆ How is a pleasure friend different from a utility friend?

◆ Do you think that a pleasure friend can turn into a true friend? How?

◆ Can you think of some examples of pleasure friends in movies or TV?

◆ Why do you think that young children only have pleasure or utility friends?

 True Friends

◆ True friends are first attracted to you because they see the good in you.

◆ There is good in everyone – the true friend is the one who can see this.

◆ A true friend is more interested in loving than in being loved.

◆ If you want to have good friends, you have to be a good friend.

◆ The true friend leaves it to the other person to return the love, and doesn't demand it. If love is demanded, it cannot be given freely.

◆ The true friend will be there for you when you are being difficult and when things go wrong. This kind of friend doesn't expect to be rewarded for doing this – it is what true friends do!

◆ For true friendship, both friends need to want good things for the other person.

◆ True friendship doesn't ever stop

◆ The friend keeps on wanting good things for the other person.

Discuss.

◆ Why do you think people try too hard to make friends?

◆ What do you think of this statement: If you want a good friend, be a good friend.

◆ Why do you most people have only a small number of true friends?

◆ How do you know that there must be something good in you?

 # Friendship Takes Time

"People are not true friends until they have eaten a bushel of salt together." - Aristotle

Aristotle didn't mean that people had to eat a big bag of salt all at once! Only a small amount is used at each meal.

It takes a very long time before a whole bag is used up.
What he meant was that people need to spend a lot of time together learning about each other before they can be true friends.

Friendship unfolds gradually.
You start with "small talk" and simple facts about yourself and you find out something about the other person.
As you feel more comfortable, you start to trust the other person, and you begin to share things that are more important to you.

Remember, not everyone you meet will be your friend. You should not tell personal secrets to someone you don't know very well.
Not everyone deserves to have special knowledge about you.

It is immature and foolish to reveal everything about yourself to someone you have just met. It makes you look "desperate".
In true friendship, you slowly explore the mystery of each other.

Discuss.

◆ Do you agree that true friendship takes time to grow?

◆ When do you know that you have a good friend?

◆ When do you know that you are a good friend?

◆ What do you think might happen if you tell too much about yourself when you first meet someone?

41

What do you remember about friendship?

(Without looking back, see if you can fill the spaces with a word that fits.)

◆ User friends _____ you for what they can get out of you.

◆ If you stop being _____, you will stop being their friend.

◆ User friends give just enough to keep the friendship going, but they are mainly interested in _____ what you have to offer them.

◆ Pleasure friends are your friends only because they find some _____ in being your friend.

◆ A pleasure friend might love some special _____ in you. If the friend stops finding it pleasurable, the friendship will stop.

◆ A pleasure friend won't let you be _____ – you have to be showing them the quality they like all the time or they won't be your friend!

◆ Most young children only have pleasure friendships. As they grow and change, so do their friendships. This is _____.

◆ Some teenagers and even some adults never grow up in the way they act towards their friends! They remain _____ and self-centred.

◆ True friends are first attracted to you because they see the _____ in you. There is good in everyone – The true friend is the one who can see this.

◆ A true friend is more interested in _____ than in being loved. If you want to have good friends, you have to be a good friend.

◆ The true friend leaves it to the other person to return the love, and doesn't demand it.

◆ If love is demanded, it cannot be given _____. The true friend will be there for you when you are being difficult and when things go wrong. This kind of friend doesn't expect to be _____ for doing this – it is what true friends do!

◆ For true friendship, both friends need to wish _____ things for the other person.

◆ True friendship doesn't ever _____ – the friend keeps on wishing good things for the other person.

◆ Aristotle said that people are not true friends until they have eaten a bushel of _____ together.

◆ People need to spend a lot of _____ together learning about each other before they can be true friends.

◆ Friendship unfolds _____.

◆ You start with _____ _____ and simple facts about yourself and you find out something about the other person.

◆ As you feel more comfortable, you start to _____ the other person, and you begin to share things that are more important to you.

◆ Remember, not everyone you meet will be your friend.

◆ You should not tell personal _____ to someone you don't know very well. Not everyone deserves to have special knowledge about you.

◆ It is _____ and foolish to reveal everything about yourself to someone you have just met. It makes you look _____.

◆ In true friendship, you slowly explore the _____ of each other.

 # Points to bring out

Purpose: To give a simple explanation of the way in which married love is like the love of God. To begin explaining that sexual intercourse is meant to be an expression of true love.

◆ Start with the box at the bottom of the page, and have your child read the contents of the box – these words are an important summary of the meaning of true love, and will be continually repeated.

◆ Tell your child that married love is meant to be a way that we can learn and grow in true love. Talk through what each of these means in marriage using the first six points on the page.

◆ You might need to mention that marriage partners aren't perfect, and they don't always succeed in doing these things – but they keep on trying, and they need to ask for God's help to make it work better.

◆ Look at the picture. Tell your child that on their wedding day, spouses promise to be true to one another for the whole of their lives. Ask them to read aloud the words beneath the picture. Recall any weddings they may have attended. (You may like to show your child your own wedding photos if they would be interested!)

◆ Talk about the dot points beside the picture:
The act of intercourse is the physical sign that two people have been joined in marriage. Like all sacraments, it is a physical sign of a spiritual reality. In married love, every act of intercourse is open to love and open to life if it is to be an act of true, God-like love.

◆ This conversation may lead to questions regarding the more intimate details of what is meant by sexual intercourse. It is preferable to finish exploring the meaning of marriage before going into this kind of detail. You may like to use the following sheet to give a brief explanation, with the promise that you will be covering this information in more detail shortly.

 Married Love

◆ When a man and woman get married, they make a **free** choice to give their love to each other.

◆ Their choice of marriage partner is **permanent** unless and until the other person dies.

◆ When they give themselves to each other they try to be **unselfish** – they think of the needs of the other person first.

◆ They set **no limits** to how much love they will give to each other.

◆ When they show love like this, they make a **gift of themselves** to each other; they are sharing God's life of love. (We call this life grace.)

◆ By doing the ordinary things involved in showing love for each other every day, they grow closer to God and to each other.

◆ Husband and wife show this love through the act of intercourse.

◆ The act of intercourse is the physical sign that two people have been joined in marriage.

◆ In married love, every act of intercourse is open to love and open to life.

What God has joined man must not divide.

"I promise to be true to you in good times and in bad; in sickness and in health; so long as we both shall live."

When we love truly, it will be the same kind of love that Jesus showed us:
Free, Permanent, Unselfish, Unlimited, Gift of self

Points to bring out

Purpose: This activity is has been added in response to requests from parents for an activity to be used if the child wishes at this point to probe more deeply on the meaning of sexual intercourse. Only use it at this point if you think your child needs it.

Otherwise, the topic can be left until the section on "Changing and Growing".

The Meaning of Sexual Intercourse
"And the two shall become one..."

When a man and woman marry, they are meant to love each other with the truest kind of love. They make a gift of themselves to each other in a way that is free, permanent, unselfish and unlimited.

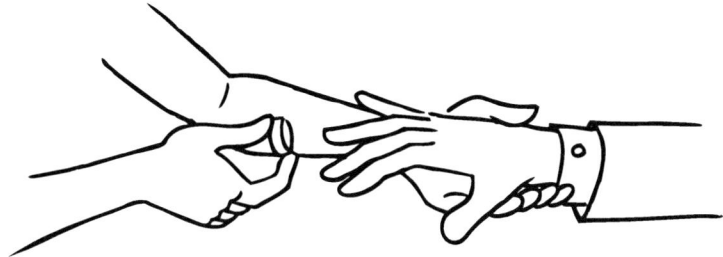

"… This is why a man leaves his father and mother and joins himself to his wife, and they become one body.
"Now both of them were naked, but they felt no shame in front of each other." Genesis 2: 24 – 25.

When they do this, God joins them together in a very special way. One way that they show this is through sexual intercourse, which is the physical (bodily) sign that they have become one. They belong only to each other and to no other human being.

During sexual intercourse, the man places his penis in the woman's vagina. (The way in which this becomes possible will be explained when you learn more about the male and female reproductive systems.)

Just like the man and woman in the book of Genesis, husband and wife can be naked in front of each other and be unashamed. All that they have and all that they are belongs to the other.

The way that they share their lives with each other prepares them for sharing with the children who are born to them.

Points to bring out

Purpose: To encourage your child to see the value and beauty of motherhood and fatherhood.
To help your child to understand the meaning of virginity and its value.

◆ Start by reading the words in bold type underneath the three pictures. Try to bring out the astonishing truth that only human beings cooperate with God in making new persons. God does not add new persons to the Trinity, and angels do not create new persons either.

◆ Read the rest of the words underneath the third picture. Explain what the word virginity means: [One who has not had sexual relations with anyone else.]

◆ Explain the value of virginity before marriage: it means that you can use your sexual powers in the way that they are meant to be used – to show true love.

◆ Ask your child to explain to you why only married people can use their sexual powers to show true love. [Answer: Only married couples can use their sexual powers in a way that is free, permanent, unselfish, unlimited and capable of sharing the life of God – grace.]

◆ Discuss the questions at the bottom of the page – be prepared to share the good things about being a parent!

Motherhood and Fatherhood

The Power to give life to a new human person is a great gift of God – a special vocation.

God doesn't add new persons to the Trinity.

Angels don't make new angels.

◆ Only human beings, in cooperation with God, give life to new persons.

◆ The vocation of mother and father is a special calling from God.

◆ Before they get married, a couple do not use their sexual powers; they save themselves for the time when they can express their love truly.

◆ This is called virginity, and those who save themselves for their true love are called virgins.

Discuss

Have you ever thought about what God is calling you to do with your life?

What would you want for your child if you became a parent?

What might be the rewards of being a parent?

What would make it hard to be a good parent?

Points to bring out

Purpose: To help children to see that marriage is not the only vocation that people can be called to.

To explain that all people are meant to express love – but sexual powers can only be used properly within marriage.

◆ Tell your child that while marriage is a beautiful way to express love as a human person, it is not the only way. Then read through the words beside the box.

◆ Tell your child that not everyone is called by God to be married. They do not become less human by doing this – after all, it is the way Jesus lived. Their celibacy gives them the time to serve God and other people in the same way that Jesus did.

◆ Look at the captions on the bottom half of the page. As you read through them with your child, ask them if they know anyone who fits in to the category that you are talking about.

Should Everyone be Married?

If marriage shows God's love, and making new persons is such a wonderful gift, shouldn't we all be married?

No. We are all called to love God in different ways.
The way God wants for us will be the best for us.

Priests and religious give of themselves through their
bodies by giving up any sexual activity.

Every human person is called by God to show love through their bodies, just as Jesus did.

**Some people show
this love in marriage.**

**Some people give
themselves to
God and don't
ever marry**

**Priests and Religious give their
lives directly to God. They do
not get married. This is called
celibacy.**

**Because they do not need to
spend time building up the life
of their own family, celibacy
allows them to spend more time
in serving God and other people.**

Points to bring out

Purpose: To help children to see that everybody was made by God for a reason; everyone has a call from God (a vocation).

To teach children that everyone is called to be holy in their own way.

To begin a conversation about your child's particular vocation.

◆ Begin by reading the scripture passage at the top of the page. Tell your child that we have been made by God for a reason. He has given us all a special vocation to come closer to him.

◆ Read the words beneath the scripture verse. Tell your child that everyone has been called by God to become holy in our own way. Only this will make us happy.

◆ [Each person has their own unique vocation. Parents should be very careful that children are not pressured to become something they are not called to. Choice of vocation takes a while to work out – it's good to start thinking about it and discussing it.]

◆ Read the words around the graphic, and then discuss the questions underneath it. The discussion points are meant to start a long and ongoing conversation. Don't stop after this session!

Vocation: My Calling in Life

"I have called you by your name. You are mine." Isaiah 43:1

Every human person is created directly by God.

God has called each one of us to become holy by following Jesus.

This call (vocation) to be holy has been given to every human person, but each of us will live it out in a different way.

God gave you a mind to help you work things out for yourself.
– Don't wait for an angel with a scroll to tell you what to think!

How will I know what my vocation is?

There will be clues to point you in the right direction:
What are your talents?
What do you believe God wants of you?
What do your family and friends think you're good at?
What are your circumstances?

**But you have to make your own decision, with the help of God.
God created you and knows what will make you truly happy.
You should pray for His guidance as you think about it!**

Think about or discuss these questions.

◆ What talents do I have?
◆ How did your parents decide on what their vocation was?
◆ What kinds of things would I be good at? (What do I really not want to do – the opposite is likely to give you a good idea of the kind of thing you would really like!)
◆ How would I know if God wanted me to be a priest or a religious sister or brother?

The Gift of Fertility

The Gift of Fertility

Girls
• Parents should follow the gradual physical development of their daughters and help them to accept the development of their femininity in a bodily and spiritual sense.

• Normally, the cycles of fertility and their meaning should be discussed.

• Girls should also have some understanding of the development that is taking place in boys during puberty.

Boys
• Boys must be helped to understand the stages of physical development of the genital organs.

• Boys should also be given some understanding of female sexual development, particularly the cycles of fertility.

• Male Reproductive System Diagram of the male reproductive system

• Female Reproductive System Diagram of the female reproductive system

• Female Reproductive System Detailed diagram of the female reproductive system

• The Menstrual/Ovulation Cycle; Fertilisation Diagram of the Menstrual/Ovulation Cycle Simple diagram of fertilisation.

·

Some helpful hints to parents.
If you are uncertain of the details and words needed to explain this subject, it would be helpful to have access to a good book on the subject. The following texts are recommended:

Sexuality Explained by Louise Kirk
Teachable Moments by Julianne Whyte & Lise Brick
The Wonder of Me by Ruth S. Taylor & Ann Nerbun
Our Power to Love by Ruth S. Taylor, Ann Nerbun & Richard M. Hogan

Points to bring out

◆ The website of the Billings Family Life Centre is highly recommended as a source of accurate information. The web address is www.woomb.org

◆ The activity presumes that parents have a basic understanding of the structure of the male reproductive system. Simply describe the main elements using the correct terms.

◆ The description should refer at least to the following elements:

Pituitary gland
Penis

Urinary   functions
bladder, urethra

Sexual functions
scrotum
testes (testicles)
vas deferns
ejaculatory ducts

# Male Reproductive System

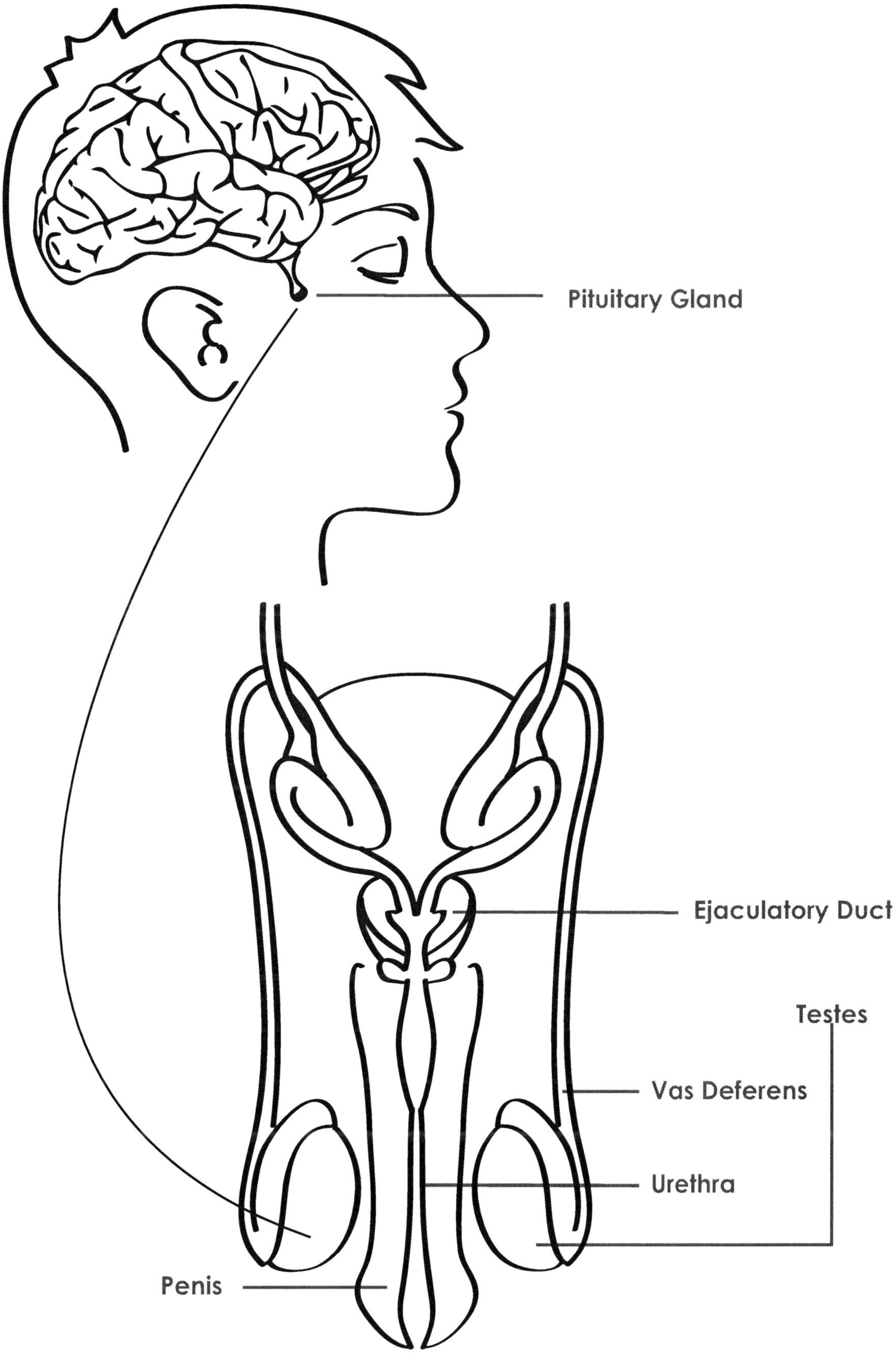

Pituitary Gland

Ejaculatory Duct

Testes

Vas Deferens

Urethra

Penis

Points to bring out

◆ The website of the Billings Family Life Centre is highly recommended as a source of accurate information. The web address is www.woomb.org

◆ The activity presumes that parents have a basic understanding of the struture of the female reproductive system. Simply describe the main elements using the correct terms.

◆ The description should refer at least to the following elements:

Urinary functions
bladder, urethra

Sexual functions
Cervix
Uterus
Fallopian tubes
Ovary
Pituitary gland
Womb
Vagina

Female Reproductive System

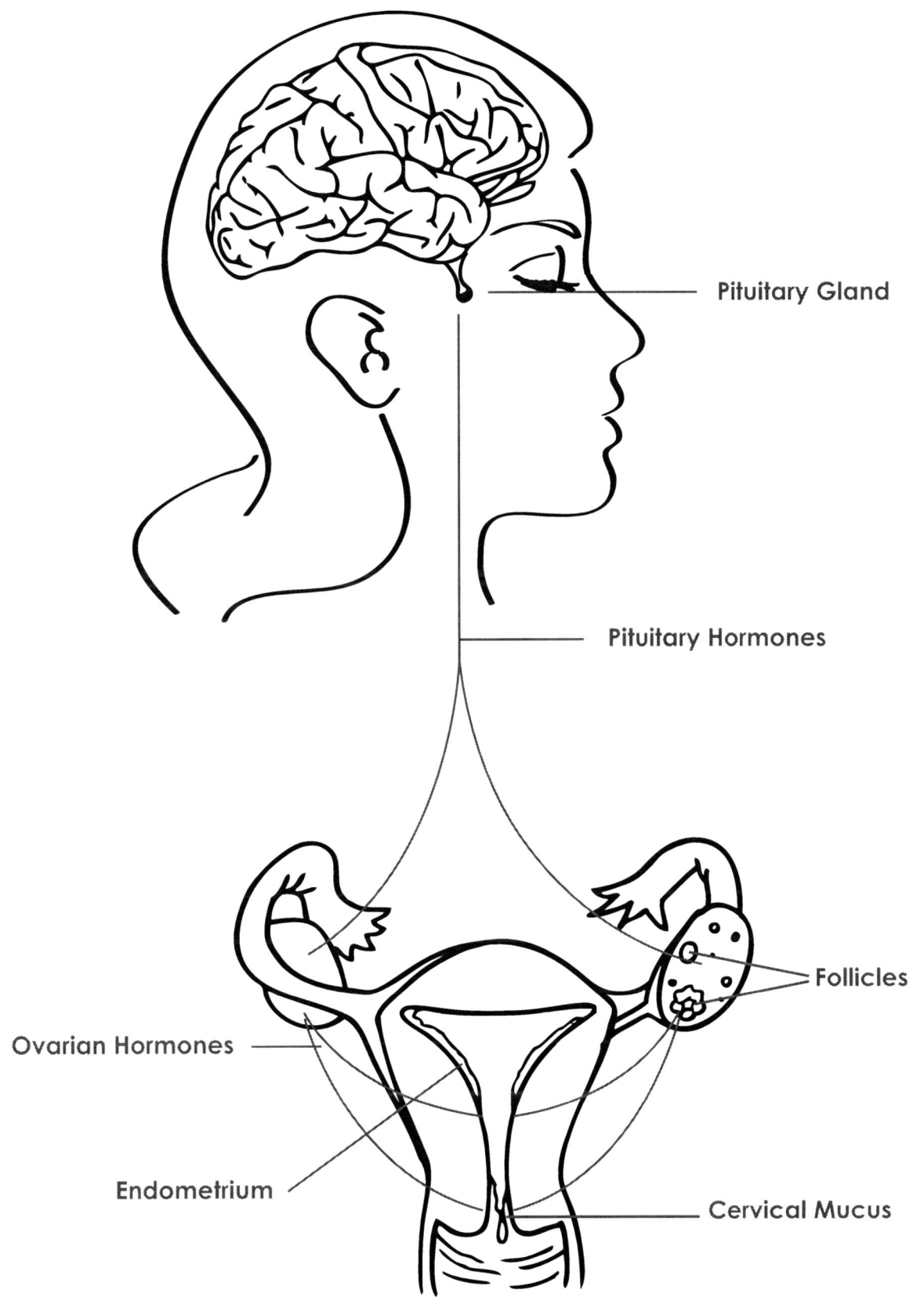

Pituitary Gland

Pituitary Hormones

Follicles

Ovarian Hormones

Endometrium

Cervical Mucus

 # Female Reproductive System (Detail)

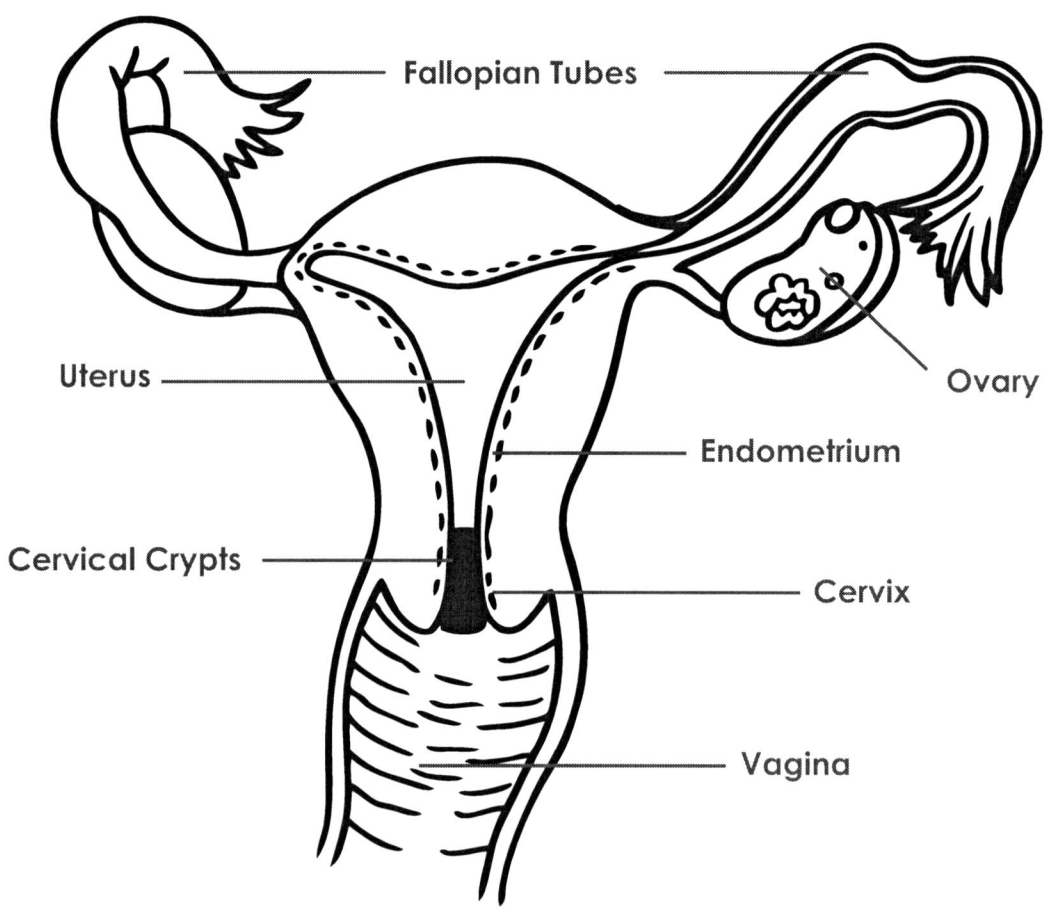

Fallopian Tubes

Ovary

Uterus

Endometrium

Cervical Crypts

Cervix

Vagina

 # Female Reproductive System (Fertilization)

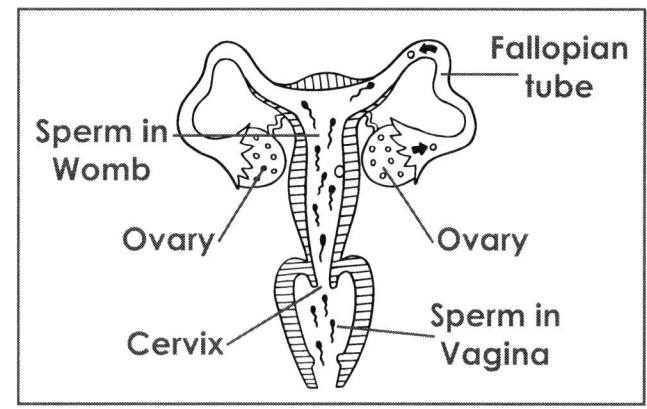

Sperm in Womb

Fallopian tube

Ovary

Ovary

Cervix

Sperm in Vagina

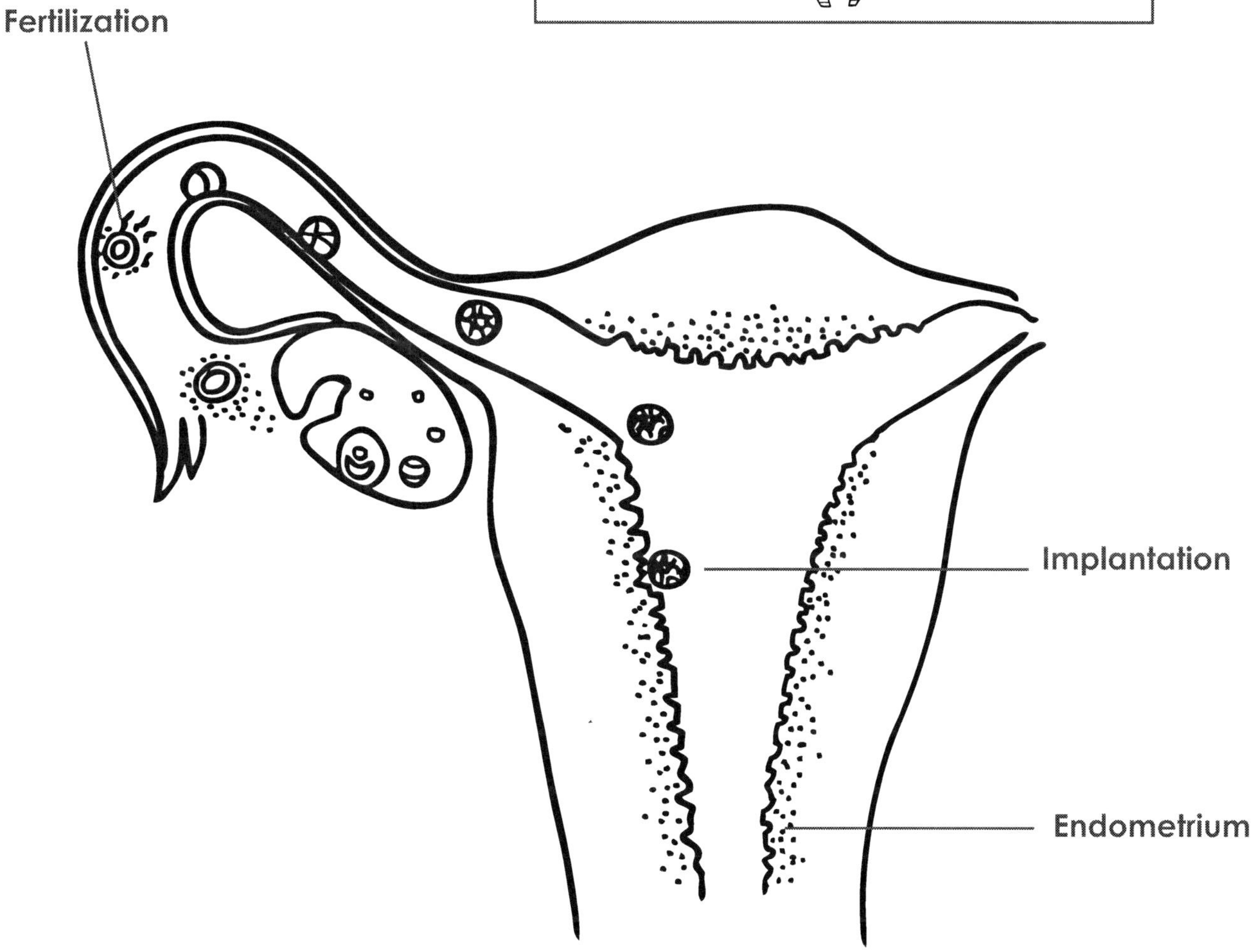

Fertilization

Implantation

Endometrium

Menstruation/Ovulation Cycle

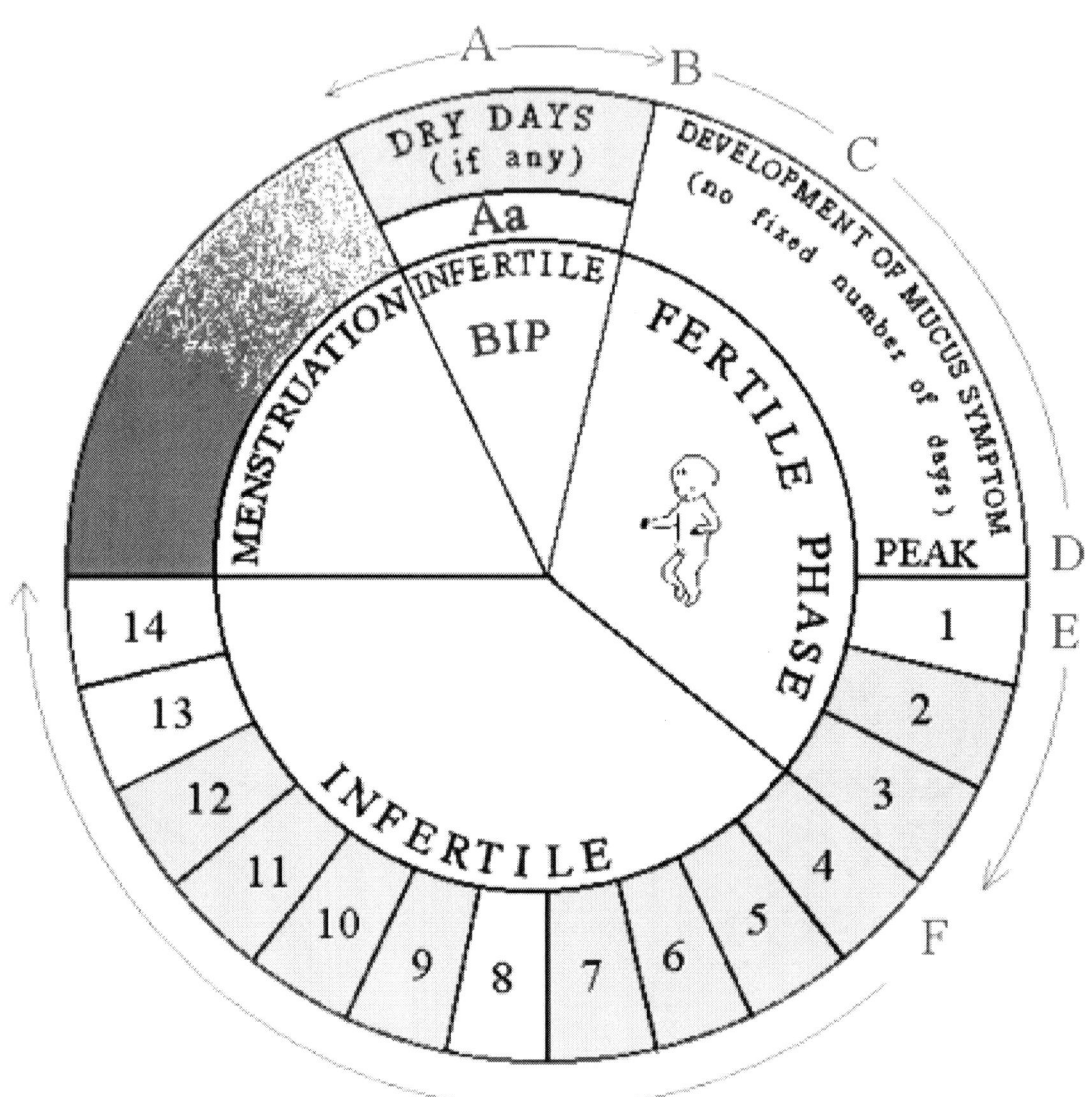

Fertilisation

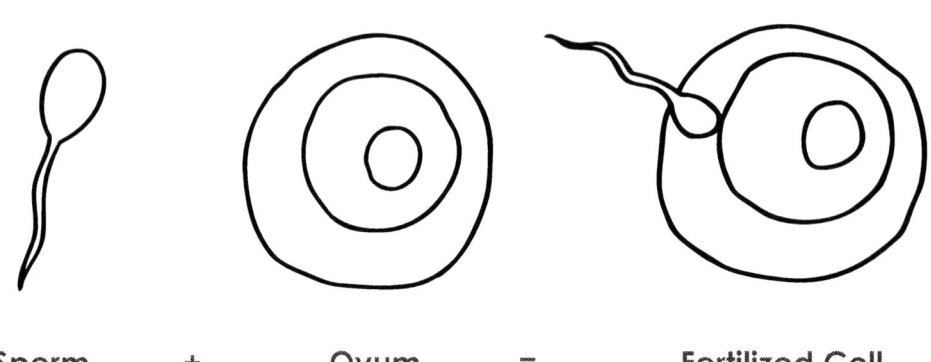

| Sperm | + | Ovum | = | Fertilized Cell (New Life) |

Faith and Ethics

Faith and Ethics

◆ *Identify and give basic explanations for the sixth and ninth commandments:*
You shall not commit adultery.
You shall not covet your neighbour's spouse.

◆ *Explain that marriage was instituted by God. The Sacrament of Marriage is exclusive and for life.*

Pure Love

◆ True love is pure love; it is not mixed with other things.
◆ Pure love is free, permanent, unselfish, has no limits and is a gift of yourself. Brief comprehension activity.

Purity in a Human Person

◆ In a human person, pure love requires the proper use of our sexual powers. This is called purity, or chastity.
◆ Every human person is called to live in chastity.

Two Commandments

◆ Two of the Ten Commandments remind us that we should live chastely.
◆ Purity prepares the soul for love.

The Sixth Commandment

◆ The sixth commandment calls us to respect our person and that of others.
◆ The sixth commandment reminds us that true love is permanent.
◆ Some ways we can strengthen our love.

Respect for Persons

◆ Comprehension activity on page 71.

The Ninth Commandment

◆ Guiding our thoughts towards pure love.
◆ Respect for family life.
◆ God never expects the impossible from us.

Respecting Family Life

◆ Comprehension activity on page 78.

Faith and Ethics

Faith and Ethics Part 1: The Nature of Love
◆ Identify and give basic explanations for the sixth and ninth commandments:
6. You shall not commit adultery.
9. You shall not covet your neighbour's spouse.

◆ Explain that marriage was instituted by God. The sacrament of Marriage is exclusive and for life.

Faith and Ethics Part 2: Good Reasons For Believing As We Do
◆ In answering children's questions, parents should give good reasons for chastity and show the weakness of theories and ideas that encourage permissive behaviour.
◆ Boys and girls at puberty are particularly vulnerable to emotional influences. Through dialogue and the way they live, parents should help their children resist negative outside influences.
◆ Parents should teach their children the value of Christian modesty, moderate dress. Parents should explain that a mature personality does not feel the need to follow every trend. - from "Truth and Meaning of Human Sexuality" [See List of Internet Articles]

Faith and Ethics Part 3: Issues To Talk Through
◆ Even if they are socially acceptable, some habits of speech and conduct are not morally correct and represent a way of trivializing sexuality, reducing it to a consumer object.
◆ Through an open dialogue, parents can guide their sons and daughters when they face emotional difficulties and support the value of Christian chastity. - from "Truth and Meaning of Human Sexuality"

Points to bring out

Purpose: To open up the subject of chastity by explaining it in terms of "pure love".
To describe the characteristics of "pure love".

◆ Begin by pointing to the two pictures at the top of the page and reading their captions. Point out that pure substances are highly prized – pure gold, pure joy, pure olive oil! It means that what we are getting is the real thing. Ask your child if he/she is aware of any other kind of pure substance that is highly prized.

◆ Tell your child that pure love is no different. The purer it is, the truer it is! Read through the characteristics of pure love that are found in the box Have your child fill in the missing words. All of the answers can be worked out from looking back through the characteristics of pure love described in the box above.

◆ Tell your child that pure love – like pure anything else – is well worth striving for!

 Pure Love

A pure substance is one that has not been mixed with anything else.

Pure joy is not mixed with any kind of sadness!

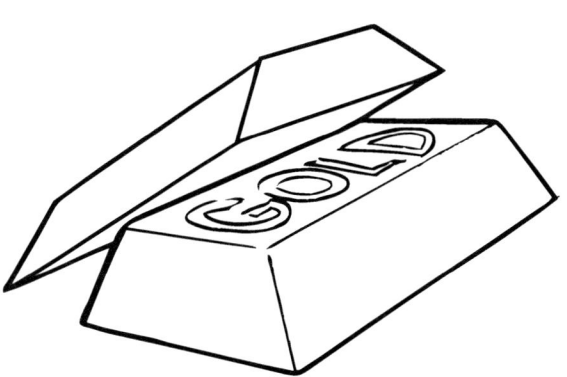

Pure gold is gold that has not been mixed with less valuable metals.

Pure love is love that is not mixed with other things...

Pure love is free – nobody can force you to love them; nor can you force them.

Pure love is permanent – it is not just for the moment; it is for always.

Pure love is unselfish – it considers the other person first.

Pure love knows no limits – it does not stop when things become difficult.

Pure love is a gift – Jesus showed us how to do this and he taught us to "love one another as I have loved you". Love makes a gift of itself to another without demanding anything in return.

Pure love requires purity (right use of our sexual powers).

Use the information in the box above to fill in the missing words...

Pure love helps me to share _____ love with others. Jesus showed us how to do this.

Pure love is _____. Nobody can force you to love them.

Pure love lasts for always – it is _____.

Pure love allows us to make a _____ of ourselves to others.

Pure love doesn't stop when things become _____.

Points to bring out

Purpose: To help the child make the connection between pure love and "purity" or "chastity".

◆ Begin by looking at the two pictures at the top of the page, and reading the captions aloud.

◆ Tell your child that human persons will show pure love in a different way from angels, because human persons have bodies and are part of the material world.

◆ Tell your child that a very important part of pure love for human persons is called "purity". Purity means using our sexual powers the right way.

◆ Read the words in bold type above the pictures in the middle of the page, then look through the pictures.

◆ Tell your child that by using our sexual powers in the right way:
We are trying to love the way Jesus showed us.
We are doing this because it will make us truly human and truly happy.
Our sexual powers were given to us by God so that we could use them to show pure love.

◆ Explain that purity is also called chastity. (Chastity is not celibacy; it is the proper use of our sexual powers. Married people have to be chaste too!)

Purity in a Human Person

When persons show pure love, they are acting the way they should.

Pure love for a human person is different from the pure love that would be right for other kinds of persons, such as angels.
It involves the right use of our sexual powers.

For a human person, purity means that our sexual powers are used as they should be – to show pure (true) love.
The right use of our sexual powers is also called chastity.
Every human person is created to live chastely – at all times and in every state of life...

Children

Teenagers

Single people

Married People

Priests

Religious

In a human person, purity involves the right use of our_____ powers.
Angels express pure love in a different way from _____ persons.
Our sexual powers are meant to help us express _____ love.
In human persons, the right use of our sexual powers is called

_____.
Every human person is created to live _____ at all times.

 # Points to bring out

Purpose: To connect the work done on purity and pure love with the positive function of the Ten Commandments.

To introduce the vocabulary that will be needed to discuss the sixth and ninth commandments.

◆ Begin by reading the words at the top of the page.

◆ Tell your child that the Commandments are not simply a list of don'ts. They remind us of what it means to be human, and tell us what kind of behaviour that will make us less than we can be.

◆ Have your child do the "Find a Word" activity. He/ she should be aware of most of the meanings. You may need to explain the following words:

Spouse: Your marriage partner.

Covet: to desire eagerly something that belongs rightfully to someone else.

◆ When you have finished read the quote from Cardinal Newman at the bottom of the page. It is a good summary of the function of purity (chastity).

# The Commandments

When persons show pure love, they are acting the way they should.

Human persons have been created to show true love. Only this will make us truly happy.

Human persons must show true love using their bodies. This involves the right use of our sexual powers – chastity.

If we don't live chastely, we will always feel uneasy about what we are doing. We will know that we can do better.

Two of the Ten Commandments remind us to live our human lives chastely…

VI. You Shall not commit adultery.
IX. You shall not covet your neighbour's spouse.

Find these words in the grid, and shade them in…
pure love; purity; chastity; chastely; happy; body; spouse; covet; neighbour.

B	P	U	R	I	T	Y	I	O	P	B	O	D	Y	G
L	K	N	T	M	N	B	V	C	X	Z	A	S	D	F
V	K	J	S	D	F	Q	W	E	J	G	M	D	Z	X
I	U	R	Y	L	E	Y	W	T	H	A	P	P	Y	V
O	B	P	U	R	E	L	O	V	E	I	T	K	V	M
J	Q	C	K	Z	W	T	R	S	I	V	S	V	W	N
O	V	D	H	Q	N	T	V	L	P	W	V	L	N	T
C	W	L	R	A	L	C	H	A	S	O	E	L	V	K
E	W	K	P	T	S	N	E	I	G	H	B	O	U	R
T	P	Z	I	S	J	T	J	N	D	Z	X	S	X	L
X	V	C	I	P	R	K	I	D	R	X	M	R	E	B
C	O	V	E	T	P	R	P	T	P	V	W	P	R	M
U	T	M	N	B	V	C	I	P	V	N	B	V	P	I
B	R	Y	L	E	V	W	V	I	V	Q	N	T	V	L
Q	K	P	T	N	Y	W	W	V	V	Q	W	L	P	B

"Purity prepares the soul for love… and love confirms the soul in purity."
Cardinal Newman.

Points to bring out

Purpose: To bring out the full meaning of the sixth commandment: our need to respect our own person and the person of others.

◆ Start by reading the first paragraph which explains what is meant by "adultery".

◆ Then read the next two sentences. Tell your child that the sixth commandment implies far more than what it actually says. Persons deserve respect and honour. So this commandment reminds us to respect ourselves and others.

◆ Tell your child that "pure love" is the only thing that can make human beings truly happy – it was what we were made for. Living in pure love is called living chastely.

◆ Let your child know that it is not always easy to live this way, but the effort is worthwhile. It requires the help of God in the ways described on the activity sheet.

◆ Read through the captions underneath each box. Think about whether or not you are making it difficult for yourself by neglecting any of these practices. These are the things that will enable us to live in pure love through the exercise of purity.

The Sixth Commandment

The sixth commandment reminds us that we are human persons.
We should have great respect for our own person and the person of others.

VI. You Shall not commit adultery.

To adulterate is to make a thing impure by mixing it with something that is not as good. If someone commits adultery in marriage, one of the partners has sexual intercourse with someone else. This makes their love for their spouse less than what it should be. Their love for each other is diluted by bringing somebody else into the relationship. This is an improper use of their sexual powers.

The sixth commandment reminds of what true love is. We are called to live in pure love, not mixing our love with selfishness.

The sixth commandment teaches us that love is permanent – in marriage this means that we are faithful to the one we have promised to love.

Every human person is called to live chastely. To do this we need to ask God's help...

Prayer
Pray for the grace of God so that we can be who we are meant to be.

Good Works
Learn to love truly by giving your time and talent to those who need your help.

Kindness & Unselfishness
Be kind and unselfish towards those who are closest to you in your own family.

"Lead us not into temptation..."
Avoid those sins that tempt you to misuse your sexual powers and make your love impure – actions, words, pictures, internet sites.

Sacrament of Penance
If you make a mistake, ask for God's forgiveness in the Sacrament of Penance (Reconciliation). God always wants to forgive you and let you start again...just ask!

The Eucharist
Increase God's own life in you through the Eucharist. It will make your true love grow and strengthen your will to love with pure love.

Points to bring out

Purpose: To explain that chastity involves more than actions; it requires an effort to guard our thoughts and words as well.

To point out the need for husbands, wives and children to respect one another.

◆ Tell your child that purity is not about actions only. Explain that the ninth commandment shows us that we cannot afford to let our thoughts and desires go too far either – they may eventually lead to actions in any case. Read the sentences at the top of the page.

◆ Have your child read the words beside the picture in the middle of the page then ask what they mean. [Answer: That we should not make excuses for ourselves. Things might seem to be hard to do, but God will help us if we ask him.]

◆ Point out to your child that there are many opportunities in our society to let our thoughts take us in the wrong direction. If you become aware that this is happening, you need to make efforts to stop. This is one area where you will need to ask for God's help directly by brief prayers.

◆ Tell your child that the ninth commandment also teaches us that we should respect family life – our own and that of others. Husbands, wives and children all need to respect each other and be loyal to one another in the way they think and speak about each other. If we are constantly "fault finding" we can never be happy. This is the family God has given you. It is up to you to love them.

The Ninth Commandment

ıX. You shall not covet your neighbour's spouse.

The ninth commandment reminds us that human persons must try to show pure love at all times – in their thoughts as well as their actions. To covet means to desire eagerly something that belongs rightfully to someone else.

These kinds of desires can only happen in our minds and imaginations, so we need to gain control over our thoughts.

The ninth commandment also teaches us to have respect for family life; our own and that of others.

God never expects the impossible from us.
He created us the way we are, and so he knows what we are capable of.

Nobody can stop thoughts from coming into their minds – but we can stop ourselves from dwelling on them or seeking them.

This is what is meant by gaining control over our thoughts. This is best done immediately – the longer you leave bad thoughts there, the harder it is to clear your mind.

Family life is God's plan for helping spouses and children to learn about true love. Husbands and wives need to respect one another and their children.

The ninth commandment reminds us to stay away from things that might tempt us to misuse our sexual powers and make our love impure.These can be actions, words, pictures, some video clips, movies or certain internet sites.

Respecting Family Life

The ninth commandment tells us You shall not _____ your neighbour's wife.

To covet means to _____ eagerly. Desires such as these can only happen in our _____, so we must understand that this commandment teaches us that we must gain control over our _____.

The ninth commandment also teaches us to respect _____ life. It is God's plan for helping spouses and _____ to learn about true _____.

Husbands, wives and _____ must respect one another.

We know that God wouldn't ask us to do things that are _____.

He created us and knows what we are _____ of.

We can't stop bad thoughts from coming into our _____. But we can stop ourselves from seeking them or _____ on them.

It is easier to move away from bad thoughts as soon as they occur to us. The longer we leave them there, the _____ it is to clear your mind.

The ninth commandment reminds us to stay away from things that might tempt us to misuse our _____ powers. These can be actions, _____, pictures, some video clips, _____ or certain _____ sites.

Some Common Questions

1. Once my children became teenagers, they didn't really want to listen to me when I had things to say about sex. How can I continue to help them?

It is important to begin the conversation early. Once the first signs of puberty become clear, the time has certainly arrived, although you may judge that in the case of particular children, you need to begin even earlier. You can follow the process in this book if you like, but your child will set the pace for you. If you leave these conversations until the teenage years, you will probably find that your children have found out information without your help.

Even when you have begun at a suitable time, you will probably find that many teens don't want to be forced to listen again to their parents opinions – you have probably been more effective than you realise and they are likely to know what you think already. You can get around that by not speaking to them directly. Talk to you spouse about what you think when you know that they are within earshot – then they will be able to hear you without being "put under the spotlight".

Another strategy is to use movies as neutral ground. You may be able to get your teen talking to you about what they think of the behaviour of the characters. If they don't want to do this directly, you can still talk to your spouse within earshot.

2. How do I help my son or daughter resist the pressure that their peers can put on them to have sex?

Discuss the subject before it becomes personal for them. Have a lot of conversations about the way in which people use others for their own satisfaction, and relate this directly to sex. Remind them often that a true friend wants what is best for the other person – not for themselves. When a friend starts pressuring you to have sex, it is time to call a halt to the friendship.

Nevertheless, it is your son or daughter who must make this call. You cannot live their lives for them, and eventually you have to trust them. They may disappoint you, but if they fail, they need to be helped and forgiven. Encourage them to use the sacrament of reconciliation and take advice from wise counsellors. You should take all of the usual precautions of a prudent parent in so far as matters lie within your control, but if you are too overbearing, you will give them an excuse to ignore you.

3. What should I do if I discover that my son or daughter is accessing pornographic magazines or internet sites?

To begin with, make your own home computer as secure as you can so that it prevents this possibility. The amount of money you will have to spend will be insignificant in comparison with what you are getting!

If somehow this material makes it into the hands of children who are still under eighteen years of age, you need to address the matter with them directly. Be careful, however, that you deal with them compassionately. Wait until you are calm. Don't condemn or threaten. The fact that you have discovered it will make them feel uncomfortable enough. Remember that this has happened through human weakness; we live in a society that surrounds our children with these temptations.

You need to be sympathetic and tell them that you understand that they may have a problem with this. Let them know that you still love them and value them – they have made a mistake and they can fix it. Advise them to go to the sacrament of reconciliation and seek advice there. Once you have dealt with it, don't refer to it again. Once your children turn eighteen, it is far more difficult to deal with this matter, and you should take advice from a wise counsellor who understands your family situation and knows your children.

4. My child has trouble making good friends. How can I help?

You can't make anybody love you. It is often the case that children cannot make friends because they don't understand that friendship is mainly about giving. Making demands on others will damage their chances of making friends. Check back through the section on Friendship that you will find in this book, and open up a discussion about what it is that is causing the problem.

Sometimes they are unable to make friends because they are mixing with peers who don't share their values and therefore they have nothing in common. If this is the case, you may need to make efforts to find and participate in family associations that do share your values so that they don't experience a numbing loneliness because they cannot fit in with the people around them.

5. Is masturbation a sin?

Yes. The Church is very clear about this. [See Catechism of the Catholic Church 2352]

You would be well advised to read this and understand what it is saying. If you want to raise the matter with your child, you may find it difficult. One strategy might be to leave the catechism open at this page in place where your child can find it – or perhaps find a suitable article to leave around. A quick search of the internet will reveal some excellent material that can be used in this way.

One of the best discoveries we can make for the whole of our lives is the value of going regularly to the sacrament of Reconciliation. Anyone can make a mistake. You need to be able to receive God's forgiveness and move on.

6. What can I do to help my child make the right choices?

Pray for them, set a good example and use the sacraments regularly yourself (especially Reconciliation and the Eucharist).

Encourage them to go about the activities and responsibilities of their lives by organising their time so that they have plenty of things to do and achieve.

Encourage them to find ways to help others:

Join in the activities of the family, school and parish;

Find friends who think like they do;

To have lots of friends by being a good friend to have.